Article 27

The Right to an Adequate Standard of Living

A Commentary on the United Nations Convention
on the Rights of the Child

Editors

André Alen, Johan Vande Lanotte, Eugeen Verhellen,
Fiona Ang, Eva Berghmans and Mieke Verheyde

Article 27

The Right to an Adequate
Standard of Living

By

Asbjørn Eide

University of Oslo

MARTINUS NIJHOFF PUBLISHERS
LEIDEN • BOSTON
2006

This book is printed on acid-free paper.

A Cataloging-in-Publication record for this book is available from the Library of Congress.

Cite as: A. Eide, "Article 27: The Right to an Adequate Standard of Living", in: A. Alen, J. Vande Lanotte, E. Verhellen, F. Ang, E. Berghmans and M. Verheyde (Eds.) *A Commentary on the United Nations Convention on the Rights of the Child* (Martinus Nijhoff Publishers, Leiden, 2006).

ISSN 1574-8626
ISBN-13: 978-90-04-14878-9
ISBN-10: 90-04-14878-7

PRINTED IN THE NETHERLANDS

CONTENTS

LIST OF ABBREVIATIONS

CCPR	International Covenant on Civil and Political Rights, adopted by the United Nations General Assembly in 1966
CEDAW	Convention on the Elimination of All Forms of Discrimination against Women, adopted by the United Nations General Assembly in 1979
CEDAW Committee	The Committee established under the CEDAW to monitor its implementation by States
CESCR	International Covenant on Economic, Social and Cultural Rights, adopted by the United Nations General Assembly in 1966
CESCR Committee	The Committee established by the United Nations Council on Economic and Social Affairs (ECOSOC) to monitor the implementation of the CESCR by States
CESCR GenCom	A general comment adopted by the CESCR Committee
CRC	Convention on the Rights of the Child, adopted by the United Nations General Assembly in 1989
CRC Committee	The Committee established under the CRC to monitor its implementation by States
CRC GenCom	A general comment adopted by the CRC Committee
PRSP	Poverty Reduction Strategy Paper
SWAp	sectorwide approaches to development
UN	United Nations
UNICEF	United Nations Children's Fund

The conventions and the documents of the Committees can be found on the website of the UN High Commissioner for Human Rights
http://www.ohchr.org/

The activities of the CRC Committee can be found on
http://www.ohchr.org/english/bodies/crc/

The General Comments of the CRC Committee can be found on
http://www.ohchr.org/english/bodies/crc/comments.htm

The General Comments of the CESCR Committee can be found on
http://www.unhchr.ch/tbs/doc.nsf

AUTHOR BIOGRAPHY

Asbjørn Eide is former Director of the Norwegian Institute of Human Rights at the University of Oslo, former Torgny Segerstedt Professor at the University of Gothenburg and is presently visiting Professor at Lund University, Sweden. He is President of the Advisory Committee on the Framework Convention on Protection of the Rights of National Minorities of the Council of Europe. He served for 20 years (until 2004) as elected member of the expert UN Sub-Commission on Promotion and Protection of Human Rights, in which capacity he prepared several studies for the United Nations (UN), one of them dealing with the right to food as a human right. He has published extensively and edited with C. Krause and A. Rosas the textbook 'Economic, Social and Cultural Rights' (The Hague, Nijhoff, 2001).

TEXT OF ARTICLE 27

ARTICLE 27

1. States Parties recognize the right of every child to a standard of living adequate for the child's physical, mental, spiritual, moral and social development.

2. The parent(s) or others responsible for the child have the primary responsibility to secure, within their abilities and financial capacities, the conditions of living necessary for the child's development.

3. States Parties, in accordance with national conditions and within their means, shall take appropriate measures to assist parents and others responsible for the child to implement this right and shall in case of need provide material assistance and support programmes, particularly with regard to nutrition, clothing and housing.

ARTICLE 27

1. Les Etats parties reconnaissent le droit de tout enfant à un niveau de vie suffisant pour permettre son développement physique, mental, spirituel, moral et social.

2. C'est aux parents ou autres personnes ayant la charge de l'enfant qu'incombe au premier chef la responsabilité d'assurer, dans les limites de leurs possibilités et de leurs moyens financiers, les conditions de vie nécessaires au développement de l'enfant.

3. Les Etats parties adoptent les mesures appropriées, compte tenu des conditions nationales et dans la mesure de leurs moyens, pour aider les parents et autres personnes ayant la charge de l'enfant à mettre en oeuvre ce droit et offrent, en cas de besoin, une assistance matérielle et des programmes d'appui, notamment en ce qui concerne l'alimentation, le vêtement et le logement.

4. States Parties shall take all appropriate measures to secure the recovery of maintenance for the child from the parents or other persons having financial responsibility for the child, both within the State Party and from abroad. In particular, where the person having financial responsibility for the child lives in a State different from that of the child, States Parties shall promote the accession to international agreements or the conclusion of such agreements, as well as the making of other appropriate arrangements.

4. Les Etats parties prennent toutes les mesures appropriées en vue d'assurer le recouvrement de la pension alimentaire de l'enfant auprès de ses parents ou des autres personnes ayant une responsabilité financière à son égard, que ce soit sur leur territoire ou à l'étranger. En particulier, pour tenir compte des cas où la personne qui a une responsabilité financière à l'égard de l'enfant vit dans un Etat autre que celui de l'enfant, les Etats parties favorisent l'adhésion à des accords internationaux ou la conclusion de tels accords ainsi que l'adoption de tous autres arrangements appropriés.

CHAPTER ONE

INTRODUCTION*

A Right of Every Child...

1. By Article 27(1), States Parties have recognized the right of every child to a standard of living adequate for the child's physical, mental, spiritual and social development. 'Every child' means everyone – girls and boys, irrespective of where they live and from whom they descend. During the drafting it was proposed to add the words 'in accordance with national conditions' between 'recognized' and 'the right of', but this was not accepted: it was felt that it would undermine the general principle.[1]

2. To make this principle a common standard of achievement is an ambitious aim in light of the conditions actually prevailing in many parts of the world. It is therefore necessary to ask who are responsible for ensuring this right, whether they take the responsibility seriously, and what possibilities they have to fulfil it. The right set out in Article 27(1) elaborates on the general principle in Article 6, which confirms the inherent right of every child to life and requires the State to ensure to the maximum extent possible the survival and development of the child. The content of the right is discussed below in Chapter III.1.[2]

... But who are Responsible?

3. The primary responsibility is by Article 27(2) placed on parents or others responsible for the child. Their responsibility is to secure the conditions of living necessary for the child's development 'within their abilities and financial capacities'. For many children this means that their right will be rather fragile: the capacity of parents and others to ensure those conditions differ enormously within countries and between countries.

---

* January 2006.
[1] S. Detrick, *A Commentary on the United Nations Convention on the Rights of the Child* (The Hague/Boston/London, Martinus Nijhoff Publishers, 1999), p. 459.
[2] *Cf. infra* No. 39 *et seq.*

4. By Article 27(3), the States Parties have undertaken an obligation to assist the parents or others responsible for the child when necessary in fulfilling that responsibility, including by facilitating access to the material conditions required such as food, clothing and housing. Under Article 27(4), the State shall also take appropriate measures to recover maintenance from defaulting parents, which is of particular importance when one of the parents lives in another country.

5. The right of the child set out in Article 27(1) is a claim which the child in the first instance can make on its parents or other persons responsible for the child, and in the second instance on the State. Not only the State but also the parents are here seen as duty-bearers. International human rights law generally places the obligations on States, not on private parties such as parents, but one important aspect of State obligations consists in the obligation to impose duties on private parties in order to protect and ensure the rights of others. In the case of Article 27 of the CRC, the obligations of the State are twofold: to ensure that parents or other guardians fulfil their responsibility towards the child, and where required to assist them in doing so.

6. Article 27 illustrates the point now generally accepted that State obligations under international human rights law exist at three levels: the obligations to respect, the obligation to protect, and the obligation to fulfil. The latter is divided into the obligation to facilitate and the obligation to provide.

At one level, the State must *respect* the primary responsibility but also the rights of the parents in regard to the upbringing of the child. The State must abstain from unwarranted interference in the relations between parents and children. This is also reflected in several of the other provisions of the CRC such as Articles 5 and 18.

The State cannot be passive, however. As reflected in Articles 3, 19 and other provisions of the CRC, the State has a *protective* responsibility towards the child if the parent's primary responsibility fails or is neglected, for whatever reason.

Beyond its protective function, the State is also obliged to *fulfil* the rights of the child by assisting the parents and others responsible. This can be done by *facilitation* of the responsibility of the parents, *e.g.* by supporting and subsidizing kindergartens, or by direct *provision*, through providing State-run schools free of charge, by social security arrangements and by direct supplies of food and housing in times of emergency.

The Family Environment

7. As expressed in its preamble, the CRC sees the family as 'the fundamental group of society and the natural environment for the growth and well-being of all its members and particularly children. It should be therefore afforded the necessary protection and assistance so that it can fully assume its responsibilities within the community'. Also in its preamble, the CRC recalls that in the Universal Declaration of Human Rights the UN has proclaimed that childhood is entitled to special care and assistance. The need to extend particular care to the child has been expressed in a wide range of other documents cited in the preamble. The Convention thus has its conception of the ideal type of setting for the upbringing of the child: a family with the will and the capability to care for the child during its many years, starting with the pregnancy and from birth to full maturity at the age of eighteen. Their will to do so is assumed to be generated by their love for their children, and their capability is assumed to arise from their formal and informal learning of the requirements of parenthood together with their efforts to generate the necessary material resources for the upbringing of the child.

8. While fortunately there are millions of families around the world that meet these ideal criteria, it cannot be overlooked that for many other millions of children the reality is very different. On the one hand, the conception of 'family' differs substantially in different cultures. While the dominant conception in developed countries is the nuclear family consisting primarily of father, mother and their children, in many other societies the family has a more extended meaning including a wider set of relatives but also with less precise identification of the persons that hold the primary responsibility for the caring and nurturing of the child.

9. The value attached to 'childhood' is also variable. The CRC sees the child as an initially highly vulnerable person in need of protection, nurturing and care who under parental guidance gradually prepares for an independent life in a social setting of rights and duties when reaching eighteen. In contrast, children have often in the past and in many places still in the present been seen as assets for use to serve their parents and for exploitation of various kinds.

10. Even under the ideal setting where the child grows up in a family with parents committed to the best of their abilities to care, protect and coach the child towards a mature life, their ability to do so is deeply affected by the resources at their disposal, both materially and in terms of their knowledge

and skills relevant to the upbringing of the child. In settings of extreme poverty, the ability of the parents to care for the children is often very low; even the time available to care for the child may be severely limited.

11. In many developing countries, the situation is different in the rural and the urban context. Poor households in rural areas, with little or no land and other resources, are struggling for survival. The mother has limited time available to care for children since she will have to cultivate the land, fetch firewood and water. Her situation is aggravated by the fact that there is little respect for her reproductive rights. She has limited possibilities to space the birth of children. Her lack of time and resources to care for the children increases their exposure to disease and high infant mortality. The frequent deaths of the children are sought compensated for by having more children. A vicious circle keeps her and the offsprings in a situation of poverty. The greatest victims are the children below five, the period of their life when they are in constant need for care which is only inadequately met. In later years, the children in poor families have increasingly to cater for themselves, to care for their siblings and to work for the livelihood of the family as a whole.

In the urban settings of poverty such as the slum areas, the problem may be different though not necessarily better: many families are constituted by single-parent households with an absent father who never was there or has left the mother and children. One of the outcomes may be the phenomenon of street children fending for themselves at great odds in the sprawling cities of the developing countries.

12. Special problems in the family environment often face children of vulnerable minorities such as many Roma communities in Europe, children within racially discriminated groups, children of some indigenous peoples such as the aborigines in Australia, or children of low cast families such as Dalits and others in South Asia.

The Social, Cultural and Political Environment: Advances and Obstacles

13. Conditions for children's development have considerably improved during the fifteen years since the adoption of the CRC and its first ratifications by States. Nearly everywhere has infant mortality decreased significantly, which indicates that their conditions of life have improved. Access to

education has substantially increased, including for girls who in many parts of the world have been seriously underrepresented in the educational system.

14. The overall picture is still depressingly bad, however. While Article 27 asserts that every child has a right to a standard of living adequate for its physical, mental, spiritual, moral and social development, the reality faced by millions of children is far removed from that ideal. The challenges to be overcome if every child shall in fact enjoy that right are enormous. The annual UNICEF publication 'The State of the World's Children' is sobering for the facts it contains, but also for the awareness it can create in terms of the need to build the capacities and harness the resources for the task.

15. On the material side, an adequate standard of living requires access for all children to adequate food and housing including water and sanitation. The 2005 edition of 'The State of the World's Children'[3] points out that in large parts of the world, such rights are violated or remain unfulfilled. Children are severely underserved of at least one of the basic goods or services that would allow them to survive, develop and thrive. Such is the situation for more than 1 billion children, nearly half the total number of children in the world as a whole. In the developing world more than one in three children does not have adequate shelter, one in five children does not have access to safe water, and one in seven has no access whatsoever to essential health services.

16. Even the basic right to life and survival is for hundreds of thousands an unfulfilled dream. Millions of children are growing up in families and communities torn apart by armed conflict. Since 1990, conflicts have directly killed as many as 3.6 million people; tragically, more than 45 per cent of these are likely to have been children. Hundreds of thousands of children are caught up in armed conflict as soldiers, are forced to become refugees or are internally displaced, suffer sexual violence, abuse and exploitation, or are victims of explosive remnants of war.

17. AIDS is already the leading cause of death worldwide for people aged 15 to 49; in 2003 alone, 2.9 million people died of AIDS and 4.8 million people were newly infected with HIV. Over 90 per cent of people currently living with HIV/AIDS are in developing countries. AIDS has a devastating impact

[3] UNICEF, State of the World's Children 2005, available at http://www.unicef.org/sowc05/english/sowc05.pdf.

on the possibility also of the children that are not themselves infected: infected parents loose their ability to care for their children and ultimately die away from them; the numbers of orphaned children has risen exponentially during the last decade.

18. While poverty, armed conflict and HIV/AIDS are not the only factors that undermine the possibilities of the child to enjoy an adequate standard of living, they have a devastating impact and constitute the greatest challenges to the aims and visions underlying the Convention on the Rights of the Child. In the worst affected countries, such as the situation in the Democratic Republic of Congo in recent years, all these factors come together to create a pandemonium of death and deprivation. But poverty takes its enormous tolls even where there is neither armed conflict nor widespread HIV/AIDS infections.[4]

19. The 2006 edition of UNICEF's '*State of the World's Children*'[5] focuses on excluded or invisible children. Children are in the report considered excluded relative to other children if they are deemed at risk of missing out on an environment that protects them from violence, abuse and exploitation, or if they are unable to access essential services and goods in a way that threatens their ability to participate fully in society in the future. Children may be excluded by their family, the community, government, civil society, the media, the private sector and other children. Exclusion is multidimensional, including deprivations of economic, social, gender, cultural and political rights, making exclusion a much broader concept than material poverty. The concept of exclusion includes the reinforcing socio-political factors that are the basis of discrimination and disadvantage within society, requiring a strong focus on the processes and agents behind deprivation to guarantee inclusion and equality of opportunity.[6]

Towards a Shared Global Responsibility?

20. It is unrealistic to assume that all States can ensure adequate standards for all children born on their territory. International cooperation is imperative.

---

[4] *Ibid.*, p. 1 (summary).
[5] UNICEF, *State of the World's Children 2006*, available at http://www.unicef.org/sowc06/english/sowc06.pdf.
[6] *Ibid.*, p. 7.

Article 4 of the CRC states that with regard to economic, social and cultural rights, States Parties shall undertake the measures required to fulfil those rights 'to the maximum extent of their available resources and, where needed, *within the framework of international co-operation*'.

21. The Millennium Development Goals, adopted by the UN General Assembly at the Summit meeting in the year 2000,[7] call for a number of goals to be achieved by the year 2015. They are all of direct relevance for the improvement of the standards under which children live.[8] The main goals are to reduce by half the proportion of people who suffer from hunger; to ensure that all boys and girls complete a full course of primary schooling: to eliminate gender disparity in primary and secondary education, to reduce by two thirds the mortality rate among children under five; to halt and begin to reverse the spread of HIV/AIDS and the incidence of malaria and other major diseases; to reduce by half the proportion of people without sustainable access to safe drinking water; to achieve a significant improvement in the lives of slum dwellers; to integrate the principles of sustainable development into country policies and programmes and reverse loss of environmental resources. For this purpose, a global partnership for development should be developed which is rule-based, predictable and non-discriminatory and includes a commitment to good governance, development and poverty reduction – nationally and internationally.

At the end of 2005, when one third of the time has passed, it is clear that the goals will not be reached unless considerably more determined efforts are made both at national and international level.

22. International cooperation requires action at several levels: one is to assist governments in developing adequate institutions, legislation and administrative measures by which parents are brought to take more adequate measures for their children, avoiding measures that are harmful and adopting those that improve the situation of their children. Another is to transfer resources and thereby expand the total amount of resources available

---

[7] For more information, see http://www.un.org/millenniumgoals.
[8] Their relevance for the standard of living of children is discussed in UNICEF, *State of the World's Children 2006, o.c.* (note 5), pp. 3–7.

to the government in their implementation of economic, social and cultural rights. A third is to renegotiate market relations (in trade, credit, investment, debt relief and others) which can expand the sources of income of less developed countries and thereby increase the ability and financial capacity of parents to ensure adequate standards of life for their children.

While the international community does assist in many ways, through the work of UNICEF, other agencies or funds or through bilateral help, there remains disagreement regarding the extent to which assistance is obligatory and to which it is a matter of charity only. This will be further discussed in Chapter IV below.

A Note on Sources

23. The primary source is the text itself, which has to be interpreted in light of the other provisions of the convention and of other internationally recognized rights. Among the secondary sources are the *travaux préparatoires* and the practice of the CRC Committee, as reflected in the general comments and the concluding observations adopted by the Committee. The practice of other international human rights bodies can also be a factor in the interpretation of the CRC.

24. Article 27 is not very precise regarding the division of responsibility between the parents and the State; nor about the allocation of responsibility for the child's development when the child is not in the custody of the parents but of somebody else. Such gaps have to be filled out by reference to other provisions of the CRC, in particular Articles 5 and 18, by other international instruments including Article 24 of the CCPR and Article 10 of the CESCR, and by the evolving practice of the CRC Committee.

25. The general comments and the concluding observations of the CRC Committee are strictly speaking not legally binding. They do not have the same legal significance as the premises of a judgment of a court, but since they express the authoritative opinion of the body entrusted by the State Parties with the task to monitor the implementation of the convention they are given high weight in the interpretation. There is no general comment directly dealing with Article 27, but most of the general comments so far adopted have a relevance for that article, in particular CRC General Comment

(GenCom) 5,[9] GenCom 7,[10] GenCom 6,[11] GenCom 3,[12] and GenCom 2.[13] Important are also the concluding observations adopted by the CRC Committee at the end of the examination of every State report.

26. Of relevance for the interpretation and application of Article 27 of the CRC is also the practice of the Committee on the International Covenant on Economic, Social and Cultural Rights (CESCR), particularly its CESCR GenCom4 on housing,[14] CESCR GenCom 7 on housing and evictions,[15] CESCR GenCom 12 on the right to food,[16] and CESCR GenCom 5 on disability.[17]

---

[9] CRC Committee, *General Comment No. 5: General Measures of Implementation* (UN Doc. CRC/GC/2003/5, 2003).

[10] CRC Committee, *General Comment No. 7: Implementing Child Rights in Early Childhood* (UN Doc. CRC/GC/2005/7, 2005).

[11] CRC Committee, *General Comment No. 6: Treatment of Unaccompanied and Separated Children Outside Their Country of Origin* (UN Doc. CRC/GC/2005/6, 2005).

[12] CRC Committee, *General Comment No. 3: HIV/AIDS and the Rights of the Child* (UN Doc. CRC/GC/2003/3, 2003).

[13] CRC Committee, *General Comment No. 2: The Role of Independent Human Rights Institutions* (UN Doc. CRC/GC/2002/2, 2002).

[14] CESCR Committee, *General Comment No. 4: The Right to Adequate Housing* (UN Doc. E/1992/23, 1994).

[15] CESCR Committee, *General Comment No. 7: The Right to Adequate Housing: Forced Evictions* (UN Doc. E/1998/22, Annex IV, 1997).

[16] CESCR Committee, *General Comment No. 12: The Right to Adequate Food* (UN Doc. E/C.12/1999/5, 1999).

[17] CESCR Committee, *General Comment No. 5: Persons with Disabilities* (UN Doc. E/1995/22, 1994).

CHAPTER TWO

RELATED INTERNATIONAL HUMAN RIGHTS PROVISIONS

1. *In General International Human Rights Law*

27. From the inception of international human rights law, the right to an adequate standard of living has been included. While it has been a right proclaimed 'for everyone', the focus is implicitly on adult persons who are assumed to take care of their families. Thus, the Universal Declaration of Human Rights (UDHR) reads in its Article 25:

1. Everyone has the right to a standard of living adequate for the health and well-being of himself and of his family, including food, clothing, housing and medical care and necessary social services, and the right to security in the event of unemployment, sickness, disability, widowhood, old age or other lack of livelihood in circumstances beyond his control.
2. Motherhood and childhood are entitled to special care and assistance. All children, whether born in or out of wedlock, shall enjoy the same social protection.

28. The right to an adequate standard of living is set out also in Article 11.1 of the CESCR:

1. The States Parties to the present Covenant recognize the right of everyone to an adequate standard of living for himself and his family, including adequate food, clothing and housing, and to the continuous improvement of living conditions. The States Parties will take appropriate steps to ensure the realization of this right, recognizing to this effect the essential importance of international co-operation based on free consent.

Protection of and assistance to the family is set out in Article 10 of the CESCR:

1. The widest possible protection and assistance should be accorded to the family, which is the natural and fundamental group unit of society, particularly for its establishment and while it is responsible for the care and education of dependent children. Marriage must be entered into with the free consent of the intending spouses.
2. Special protection should be accorded to mothers during a reasonable period before and after childbirth. During such period working mothers should be accorded paid leave or leave with adequate social security benefits.

3. Special measures of protection and assistance should be taken on behalf of all children and young persons without any discrimination for reasons of parentage or other conditions.

29. Relevant is also Article 24(1) of the International Covenant on Civil and Political Rights (CCPR):

1. Every child shall have, without any discrimination as to race, colour, sex, language, religion, national or social origin, property or birth, the right to such measures of protection as are required by his status as a minor, on the part of his family, society and the State.

Article 23 of the CCPR, on the protection of the family, provides in Article 23(4) that in the case of dissolution, provision shall be made for the necessary protection of any children.

2. Regional Instruments on Standard of Living, Social Security and Protection of the Family

30. Article 18(2) of the African Charter on Human and Peoples' Rights sets out the obligation of States to assist the family:

The family shall be the natural unit and basis of society. It shall be protected by the State which shall take care of its physical health and moral.

The State shall have the duty to assist the family which is the custodian of morals and traditional values recognized by the community.

The State shall ensure the elimination of every discrimination against women and also ensure the protection of the rights of women and the child as stipulated in international declarations and conventions.

The aged and the disabled shall also have the right to special measures of protection in keeping with their physical or moral needs.

31. In the European Social Charter, relevant provisions are found in Article 12 (social security), Article 13 (social and medical assistance), Article 14 (right to benefit from social welfare services), and Article 16 (right of the family to social, legal and economic protection).

32. The San Salvador Protocol Additional to the American Convention on Human Rights has relevant provisions in Article 9 (social security), Article 11 (healthy environment), and Article 12 (right to food).

3. *Related CRC Articles*

33. The substantive articles of the CRC form an interdependent and indivisible whole. Article 27, like all other substantive articles in CRC, must be interpreted in light of the general principles underpinning the Convention as a whole: Article 2, requiring that States must respect and ensure all rights for every child within their jurisdiction without discrimination of any kind; Article 3 that the best interest of the child shall be the primary consideration in all action concerning children, Article 6 on the right of the child to survival and development, and Article 12 on respecting the views of the child.

34. Article 4 provides the general entry point regarding State obligations to implement the substantive rights, and Article 5 provides general guidance concerning parental responsibility in relation to the child's evolving capacities.

35. Important for the interpretation of Article 27(2) is the provision of Article 18 that parents have common responsibility for the upbringing and development of the child, while Article 19 requires the State to protect the child against abuse and neglect while in the care of parents or other primary caregivers.

36. Relevant are also Article 20 on protection of children deprived of their family environment, Article 21 on safeguards concerning adoption; Article 22 on refugee children and asylum seekers, Article 23 on the rights of disabled to special care, Article 24 on the right of children to the highest attainable standard of health, Article 26 on social security, Articles 28 and 29 on education, Article 30 on the rights of children of minorities and indigenous peoples to preserve their identity and culture, Article 31 on the right of the child to rest, leisure and play, Article 32 on protection of the child from exploitation and harmful work, Article 34 on protection against sexual exploitation, Article 35 on protection against trafficking of children, and Article 36 on protection against all other forms of exploitation prejudicial to the child's welfare.

4. *Regional Instruments Addressing the Rights of the Child*

37. The African Charter on the Rights and Welfare of the Child, adopted in July 1990 is inspired by the CRC. Its Article 20 deals with parental responsibilities:

1. Parents or other persons responsible for the child shall have the primary responsibility of the upbringing and development the child and shall have the duty:
   (a) to ensure that the best interests of the child are their basic concern at all times –
   (b) to secure, within their abilities and financial capacities, conditions of living necessary to the child's development; and
   (c) to ensure that domestic discipline is administered with humanity and in a manner consistent with the inherent dignity of the child.

2. States Parties to the present Charter shall in accordance with their means and national conditions the all appropriate measures;
   (a) to assist parents and other persons responsible for the child and in case of need provide material assistance and support programmes particularly with regard to nutrition, health, education, clothing and housing;
   (b) to assist parents and others responsible for the child in the performance of child-rearing and ensure the development of institutions responsible for providing care of children; and
   (c) to ensure that the children of working parents are provided with care services and facilities.

38. Article 17 of the European Social Charter (right of children and young persons to social, legal and economic protection) reads:

With a view to ensuring the effective exercise of the right of children and young persons to grow up in an environment which encourages the full development of their personality and of their physical and mental capacities, the Parties undertake, either directly or in co-operation with public and private organisations, to take all appropriate and necessary measures designed:

1. (a) to ensure that children and young persons, taking account of the rights and duties of their parents, have the care, the assistance, the education and the training they need, in particular by providing for the establishment or maintenance of institutions and services sufficient and adequate for this purpose;
   (b) to protect children and young persons against negligence, violence or exploitation;
   (c) to provide protection and special aid from the state for children and young persons temporarily or definitively deprived of their family's support;

2. to provide to children and young persons a free primary and secondary education as well as to encourage regular attendance at schools.

CHAPTER THREE

INTERPRETATION AND APPLICATION OF ARTICLE 27

1. *Article 27(1): Scope and Content of the Right*

39. Article 27(1) reads: '[. . .] the right of the child to a standard of living adequate for the child's physical, mental, spiritual, moral and social development'.

40. As noted in Chapter II, the right to an adequate standard of living is contained also in the Article 25 of the UDHR and Article 11 of the CESCR.[18] The term in Article 25 of the UDHR is 'adequate for the health and well-being of himself and of his family' and it includes 'food, clothing, housing and medical care and necessary social services, and the right to security in the event of unemployment, sickness, disability, widowhood, old age or other lack of livelihood in circumstances beyond his control'. Article 11 of the CESCR includes 'adequate food, clothing and housing', while the right to the highest attainable standard of health including medical care in the CESCR is placed in Article 12.

There is no further definition within any of these instruments of what the term 'adequate standard of living' should mean, but the CESCR Committee has sought to clarify the content of the right to adequate housing and the right to adequate food, which are two key components of the right to an adequate standard of living.

41. By its General Comment 4, adopted in 1991, the CESCR Committee has elaborated on the concept of an adequate standard of living in regard to housing. The Committee holds that adequate housing requires sustainable access to natural and common resources, safe drinking water, energy for cooking, heating and lighting, sanitation and washing facilities, means of food storage, refuse disposal, site drainage and emergency services.[19]

---

[18] *Cf. supra* No. 27–28.
[19] CESCR Committee, *General Comment No. 4, o.c.* (note 14), para. 8(b).

Adequate housing must also be habitable, in terms of providing the inhabitants with adequate space and protecting them from cold, damp, heat, rain, wind or other threats to health, structural hazards, and disease vectors, and the physical safety of occupants must be guaranteed as well.[20]

Adequate housing must furthermore be in a location which allows access to employment options, health-care services, schools, child-care centres and other social facilities. This is true both in large cities and in rural areas where the temporal and financial costs of getting to and from the place of work can place excessive demands upon the budgets of poor households. Similarly, housing should not be built on polluted sites nor in immediate proximity to pollution sources that threaten the right to health of the inhabitants.[21] All of the above are relevant also to determine whether the housing standards are sufficient to guarantee to the child the adequate conditions for its development.

42. In its General Comment No. 12, the CESCR Committee has defined the adequate standard regarding food as follows:

> 'The right to adequate food is realized when every man, woman and child, alone or in community with others, has physical and economic access at all times to adequate food or means for its procurement. The right to adequate food shall therefore not be interpreted in a narrow or restrictive sense which equates it with a minimum package of calories, proteins and other specific nutrients'.[22] The Committee further points out that the core content of the right to adequate food implies the availability of food in a quantity and quality sufficient to satisfy the dietary needs of individuals, free from adverse substances, and acceptable within a given culture. Dietary needs implies that the diet as a whole contains a mix of nutrients for physical and mental growth, development and maintenance, and physical activity that is in compliance with human physiological needs at all stages throughout the life cycle and according to gender and occupation.'

The CESCR Committee also points out also that the food must be both available and accessible. The latter has two dimensions: an economic and a physical one. The economic accessibility depends on the situation of the parents or guardians, see further below. Physical accessibility, according to the Committee, implies that adequate food must be accessible to everyone,

---

[20] *Ibid.*, para. 8(d).
[21] *Ibid.*, para. 8(f).
[22] CESCR Committee, *General Comment No. 12, o.c.* (note 16), para. 6.

including physically vulnerable individuals, such as infants and young children.[23]

43. Article 27 of the CRC focuses specifically on the rights of the child, and it is broader in scope than Article 11 of the CESCR. The right of the child to an adequate standard of living goes beyond the purely material aspects of living such as food and housing. The standards, or the conditions under which the child lives, must be adequate for the child's physical, mental, spiritual, moral and social development. It goes beyond the right of the child to survive by having the basic needs safeguarded. The child is entitled to enjoy conditions which facilitate its development into a fully capable and well functioning adult person.

The human species stands out from other species with regard to the long time it takes from the birth of child to the time when it can take care of itself and its own offspring. The CRC has set the end of childhood at eighteen years.[24] During those eighteen years, the development of the child goes through several stages, and the nature of the conditions necessary to facilitate the child's development varies considerably during those stages, from infant to under-five early childhood, the age of primary school and the period of adolescence.

While the conditions for the development of the child initially is almost completely set by its parents or guardians, it is later affected by and benefits from other institutions such as kindergartens, schools, later also sports clubs, religious institutions, and other associations or networks, whether within the civil society or through governmental institutions.

44. Throughout childhood, the child needs care and stimulation, but this is particularly important during the early years. The clearest example is the period of infant feeding, when the access to food is intimately related to the care and the physical proximity of the mother through breastfeeding. Not only is breastfeeding during infancy a guarantee for adequate food which meets the dietary needs of the child, but it is also essential for the care by which the child develops its sense of security and trust.[25]

---

[23] *Ibid.*, para. 13.
[24] Article 1 of the CRC.
[25] For more information: A. Eide and W.B. Eide, 'Article 24: The Right to Health', in: A. Alen, J. Vande Lanotte, E. Verhellen, F. Ang, E. Berghmans and M. Verheyde (eds.), *A Commentary on the United Nations Convention on the Rights of the Child* (Leiden, Martinus Nijhoff Publishers, 2006).

During the period of infancy, the physical development is dependent on intimate stimulation and care. The early stages also the spiritual and moral developments depend almost exclusively on the stimulation and care of the parents. As discussed below, this requires resources by the parents both in terms of time and capabilities. Gradually others become involved, through relatives and neighbouring children, the local community, the kindergarten where it exists, and later the school.

The CRC Committee has adopted a General Comment on the Implementation of Child Rights in Early Childhood (from birth to the age of eight years)[26] and another on Adolescent Health.[27] The Committee holds that already during early childhood, children should be recognized as active members of families, communities and societies, with their own concerns, interests and points of view. For the exercise of their rights, young children have particular requirements for physical nurturance, emotional care and sensitive guidance, as well as for time and space for social play, exploration and learning. While ensuring that survival and physical health are priorities, the CRC Committee points out that a young child's health and psychosocial well-being are in many respects interdependent. Both may be put at risk by adverse living conditions, neglect, insensitive or abusive treatment and restricted opportunities for realizing human potential. The survival and development of the child requires that the provisions of the CRC are implemented in a holistic manner, through the enforcement of all provisions of the Convention, including the rights to health, adequate nutrition, social security, an adequate standard of living, a healthy and safe environment, education and play as well as through respect for the responsibilities of parents and the provision of assistance and quality services. From an early age, children should themselves be included in activities promoting good nutrition and a healthy and disease-preventing lifestyle.[28]

45. In its General Comment on Adolescent Health and Development in the light of the CRC, the Committee has pointed out that adolescence is a 'period characterized by rapid physical, cognitive and social changes, including sexual and reproductive maturation'.[29] The child gradually builds up 'the capacity

---

[26] CRC Committee, *General Comment No. 7, o.c.* (note 10).
[27] CRC Committee, *General Comment No. 4: Adolescent Health and Development in the Context of the Convention on the Rights of the Child* (UN Doc. CRC/GC/2003/4, 2003).
[28] CRC Committee, *General Comment No. 7, o.c.* (note 10), para. 10.
[29] CRC Committee, *General Comment No. 4, o.c.* (note 28), para. 2.

to assume adult behaviours and roles involving new responsibilities requiring new knowledge and skills.'[30] Adolescence poses 'new challenges to health and development owing to their relative vulnerability and pressure from society, including peers, to adopt risky health behaviour. These challenges include developing an individual identity and dealing with one's sexuality. The dynamic transition period to adulthood is also generally a period of positive changes, prompted by the significant capacity of adolescents to learn rapidly, to experience new and diverse situations, to develop and use critical thinking, to familiarize themselves with freedom, to be creative and to socialize.'[31]

2. Article 27(2): Parents' Responsibility – and that of Custodians or Guardians

46. Article 27(2) provides that '[t]he parent(s) or others responsible for the child have the primary responsibility to secure, within their abilities and financial capacities, the conditions of living necessary for the child's development.'

47. The term 'primary responsibility of parents' is used also in Article 18. In her examination of the *travaux préparatoires* regarding Article 18, S. Detrick has drawn the conclusion that the choice of the term 'primary responsibility' was intended to achieve two aims:

> 'On the one hand, it was meant to protect parents or, as the case may be, other persons responsible for the child against excessive State intervention. On the other hand it was meant to indicate that parents or, as the case may be, other persons responsible for the child could not expect the State always to intervene, because the provision of the conditions of living necessary for the child's development is primarily their responsibility. That being said, the use of the term 'primary responsibility' in Article 27.2 implies that a 'secondary responsibility' to secure the conditions of living necessary for the child's development lies with the State.'[32]

48. The first implication of Article 27(2) is that parents do have a responsibility towards the child – the CRC treats the relationship between the child and parents as one of right-holders (the child) and duty-holders (the parents). The other implication, which follows from Article 18 and to some extent

[30] *Ibid.*
[31] *Ibid.*
[32] S. Detrick, *o.c.* (note 1), p. 459.

from Article 5, is that the State shall respect the primary responsibility of the parents. The State shall not intervene directly in the exercise of that responsibility unless it is necessary due to neglect or exploitation of the child, or when the parents so demand. The State can, however, offer assistance to the parents and others responsible for the child, and is to some extent obliged to do so.

49. Parents' responsibility towards their children is therefore the first issue to be discussed and clarified. Admittedly, international human rights law is generally considered to be addressed to States, not to private actors such as parents. The consequences of this conception should not be overextended, however. International human rights can set at least moral duties also for private actors. Normally international human rights law does not in itself contain obligations that are legally binding on non-State actors until implemented by national legislation, but some of them contain standards which private parties are expected to respect and apply. Article 27(2) is clearly an example. The parents do have a responsibility, and they must implement it – they cannot rely on the State to do what they should do. This follows also from the second sentence of Article 18(1): 'Parents or, as the case may be, legal guardians have the primary responsibility for the upbringing and development of the child'. States Parties have an obligation to provide assistance, however, including quality child care services.[33]

Non-State actors, including parents or others responsible for the child, are not subjected to international monitoring concerning the implementation of their responsibility. Only States are, so far, subject to monitoring or to international complaint mechanisms. On the other hand, international human rights law requires the State to adopt the necessary measures to ensure that parents or others responsible for the child fulfil their responsibility, while avoiding excessive intervention into the child/parent relationship.

50. It could be said that in the State/parent relationship the parents have a 'wide margin of appreciation' vis-à-vis the State concerning the ways in which their responsibility towards the child should be implemented, but that margin is not unlimited; the State has an explicit duty to protect the child. There is, for instance, an explicit duty of the State to intervene if the child is subject to violence, injury or abuse, neglect or negligent treatment,

---

[33] Cf. infra No. 72–75.

maltreatment or exploitation, including sexual abuse, while in the care of parent(s), legal guardian(s) or any other person who has the care of the child (Article 19(1)). Related duties of protection of the child, also against harm by its own parents, are found in Articles 32, 33 and 34. These are the outer limits of the respect that should be shown to the parents: what the parents or others responsible should not do towards the child.

The details of parental responsibility are otherwise not set out in Article 27 nor in other provisions of the CRC. Many States have formulated national requirements to the parents in specific laws intended to protect the children and to promote conditions for their adequate standard of living. A comparative study of such national laws could give considerable insight into what is expected from parents. This will not be done here, however – the subsequent discussion is limited to an interpretation of the words contained in Article 27(2) in light of other provisions in the CRC and from the practice of the CRC Committee, as expressed in its general comments and concluding observations,

2.1 'Ensuring conditions of Living Necessary for the Child's Development'

51. The parents normally play the main role in the realisation of the rights of their children. Other members of the family, including grandparents and the extended family, sometimes play important supplementary roles or in special cases even function as substitutes for one or both of the parents. The preamble to the Convention refers to the family as 'the fundamental group of society and the natural environment for the growth and well-being of all its members and particularly children'. The CRC Committee has noted that 'family' refers to a variety of arrangements that can provide for young children's care, nurturance and development, including nuclear family, extended family and other traditional and modern community-based arrangements, provided these are consistent with children's rights and best interests'.[34]

52. The 'conditions' mentioned in Article 27(2) refer to all aspects mentioned in Article 27(1): they must be adequate for the child's physical, mental, spiritual, moral and social development. The parents or other caregivers have to secure the material living conditions (food, housing, and clothing) necessary for an adequate development of the child, and must care for and

---

[34] CRC Committee, *General Comment No. 7, o.c.* (note 10), para. 15.

nurture the child already from the time of pregnancy. Above all is it important to ensure that the pregnant woman has adequate nutrition, since under- or malnutrition during pregnancy can seriously affect the future life of the child. Abstention from smoking and drugs during pregnancy is also an essential of the responsibility of the parents-to-be. During at least the first six months after birth it is also essential that the child is breastfed by the mother wherever possible. This is essential not only for as the best possible nutrition of the child and the building up immunity from illnesses, but it is also important for the intimate care required for the infant.[35]

53. Parents' care for the child is particularly important during the early childhood. 'Young children form strong emotional attachments to their parents or other caregivers, from whom they seek and require nurturance, care, guidance and protection, in ways that is respectful of their individuality and growing capacities'.[36] The CRC Committee points out that a young child's earliest years are the foundation for their physical and mental health, emotional security, cultural and personal identity, and developing competencies. During the period from infancy to the beginning of school age, the young children experience a rapid period of growth and change. Their body and nervous system develops intensely during this period, and they expand their skills and capacities of communication.[37]

Parents' responsibility goes beyond the purely physical and material. They are also required to stimulate and be the initial guide the child's mental, spiritual, moral and social development. They are the children's first educators, and should make the family an adequate environment for the early developments in these areas, as set out in Article 5 of the CRC. It is essential that parents and others in the immediate environment of the child encourages the child's dignity, self-esteem and self-confidence.

As the child grows older, others become involved including other members of the family and local community and where relevant also the staff of kindergarten or other institutions dealing with the child. While these are likely to have a considerable impact on the child's mental, spiritual, moral and social development and therefore are complementary to the parents' own efforts, the primary responsibility of the parents should wherever possible remain until the child becomes an adult at the age of 18.

---

[35] See in general A. Eide and W.B. Eide, *l.c.* (note 25).
[36] CRC Committee, *General Comment No. 7, o.c.* (note 10), para. 6(b).
[37] *Ibid.*, para. 6.

54. Of particular importance as complements to the parents' responsibility regarding the mental, moral and social developments of the child are the institutions for play and education, in particular pre-school and primary school institutions. As stated in Article 29(1)(a) of the CRC, education should contribute to the development of 'the child's personality, talents and mental and physical abilities to their fullest potential'. In the early years, *e.g.* from the age of four, care should increasingly be fused with play and education. The CRC Committee has referred to the term the concept of '*educare*' to signal a shift towards integrated services, and to reinforce the need for a coordinated, holistic, multi-sectoral approach to early childhood.[38]

55. A significant aspect of parents' responsibility is to ensure non-discrimination within the household. There must be equal access by girls and boys to food and living conditions, and equal opportunity of play and leisure. There should be no discrimination in children's participation in household chores and work in the farm and related activities, and the same opportunity to education and stimulation for tasks of various kind.

Equal opportunity for development should also be ensured for the disabled child. Special measures need to be adopted within the family to create equal opportunities for the disabled child.

Of particular importance, because it is often violated, is that there should be no discrimination between 'own' and 'other' children in the household. The issue arises when some are stepchildren, *e.g.* as a result of divorce or after the death of one of the parents, where some members of the household are the common offspring of the parents whereas others are not. The principle of non-discrimination is essential also in relation to foster-children, those who have been taken care of by others than the natural parents (*e.g.* children of poor relatives). Unfortunately such children are often put to work in the household or in the farm or other economic activities while the own children of the parents are given more time and possibility to education and plat.

2.2 'Within their Abilities'

56. Not all parents are able and possibly not even willing to fulfil all aspects of their responsibility as set out above. The CRC recognizes that parents' abilities and financial capacities vary enormously.

---

[38] *Ibid.*, para. 25.

57. Parental skills in fulfilling properly their responsibilities are sometimes limited through lack of adequate education and knowledge concerning the needs of the child. The educational skills acquired their own childhood and adult life is an essential factor in their own ability to meet the needs of their children.

58. Serious difficulties are likely to arise when the mother herself still is a child (below 18) when she gives birth. Child marriages are therefore not only a serious problem for the woman who is made to marry early, but also for the child she gives birth to. The problem of child marriage remains widespread in the poorer part of the population, particularly in rural areas in South Asia and in sub-Saharan Africa. While increasingly prohibited by laws of those countries, the laws are not effectively implemented. UNICEF's report 'The State of the World's Children' 2006 reports that nearly half of married women in rural areas in South Asia and sub-Saharan Africa were married before the age of eighteen. The negative consequences are enormous. Generally speaking, children below 18 have limited ability to care for their own children. What makes matters even worse is that when a young girl gives birth, there is a high risk of complications. Teenage pregnancies are risky, and the younger the girl, the higher the risk. Girls under 15 are five times more likely to die in childbirth than women in their twenties. Many of those who survive days of obstructed labour end up with obstetric fistula, an extremely harmful complication during childbirth with lifelong consequences.[39]

59. The ability to care for the young child depends also on the time that can be devoted by the parents, in practice particularly by the mother. In the poorer parts of the population, the mother has very many pressures on her time: in the rural areas she is expected to work at the farm, collect wood and fetch water as well as to prepare the food. If, in addition, she has several small children to attend to, the amount of time available to the individual young child is sometimes much less than what is required.

60. This is aggravated by the fact that in some sections of society she has very little protection of her reproductive rights – her knowledge of or access to contraception is limited and possibly not accepted by the husband. Her ability to space the children is therefore severely restricted. As a consequence, her ability to tend to the needs of the young children she has born is insufficient. An essential contribution to rectify this situation is to expand

---

[39] UNICEF, *State of the World's Children 2006, o.c.* (note 5), p. 47.

the access of girls not only to primary but also secondary education. This will increase not only her knowledge in general on what is the best care for the child, but will also give her better control of her reproductive rights, more knowledge of and hopefully better access to contraception, thereby also facilitating better spacing of children and ensure more time both for herself and the father to care for each of the children.

61. Where both parents are working, they can clearly not have the ability to provide adequate care to the children by themselves; access to appropriate and affordable child care institutions are therefore essential.

2.3   Caring and Guiding in accordance with the Expanding Capabilities of the Child

62. As the child grows older, its capacities expand. In their efforts to ensure the conditions for the child's development, the parents or other primary caregivers must take into account the evolving capacities of the child, as set out in Article 5 of the CRC. The child progressively acquires knowledge, understanding and expands it cognitive capacity as part of its development. The role of the parents and other caregivers is increasingly to ensure the enabling conditions by which this process of maturation can take place. These enabling conditions include the physical and material side (such as adequate housing, food and clothing) as well as the mental and moral side.

The CRC Committee has pointed out that for the realisation of rights, it is crucial to respect children's evolving capacities. It is especially significant during early childhood, because of the rapid transformations in children's physical, cognitive, social and emotional functioning, from earliest infancy to the beginnings of schooling. The parents or others responsible for the child should nurture and respect those expanding capabilities. In line with Article 12 of the CRC, the child should be allowed and even encouraged to express its own views concerning her or his development. This should be given attention and taken into account from the first years of their life: 'Young children are acutely sensitive to their surroundings and very rapidly acquire understanding of the people, places and routines in their lives, along with awareness of their own unique identity. They make choices and communicate their feelings, ideas and wishes in numerous ways, long before they are able to communicate through the conventions of spoken or written language.'[40]

---

[40] CRC Committee, *General Comment No. 7, o.c.* (note 10), para. 14.

Enabling conditions for the child's mental, moral and social development also requires that parents must listen to their young children and respect their dignity and their individual points of view. The term 'evolving capacities' in Article 5 of the CRC refers to processes of maturation and learning whereby children progressively acquire knowledge, competencies and understanding; including acquiring understanding about their rights, and about how these can best be realized. Respecting young children's evolving capacities is crucial for the realisation of rights, and especially significant during early childhood, because of the rapid transformations in children's physical, cognitive and social development. Article 5 endorses the principle that parents (and others) have responsibility to adjust continually the levels of direction, support, scaffolding and guidance they offer to a child. These adjustments take account of a child's interests and wishes as well as the child's capacities for autonomous decision making and comprehension of best interests.[41]

2.4 'Within their Financial Capacity'

63. Millions of parents are too poor to ensure an adequate standard of living for the development of their children. The causes of their poverty vary enormously: some have been irresponsible in their own use of resources, others have become impoverished due to social and economic developments over which they had no control, and yet others are themselves been born into poverty and have very little opportunity to escape out of it.

What can be demanded from the parents and other primary caregivers is that they ensure to the maximum of their available resources the material conditions for the development of the child. When, in spite of such efforts, they are unable to ensure such conditions, the State has an obligation to assist.[42] It may also be argued that the international community has an obligation to assist.[43]

---

[41] *Ibid.*
[42] *Cf. infra* No. 72 *et seq.*
[43] *Cf. infra* Chapter Four (No. 99 *et seq.*).

2.5   A Shared Responsibility

64. Parents have a shared responsibility to ensure the development of the child (Article 18 of the CRC). This responsibility extends not only to the material side (contributing to adequate housing, food and clothing) but also to the other aspects of the care and nurture due to the child. It is essential here to remind of Article 5 of the Convention on the Elimination of All Forms of Discrimination against Women (CEDAW), which requires the State to take appropriate measures to modify the social and cultural patterns of conduct of men and women, with a view to achieving the elimination of prejudices and customary and all other practices which are based on the idea of the inferiority or the superiority of either of the sexes or on stereo-typed roles for men and women. The care of the child must not be treated as a burden only on the mother; equal involvement by the father is essential. The two parents should equally function as caregivers and have an equal duty to contribute to the upbringing of the child.

65. When parents are divorced and live physically separated, efforts should be made to ensure the continued responsibility of both. The minimum duty is to ensure that both contribute to the material maintenance of the child, but as far as possible both parents should also be involved in ensuring enabling conditions for the child's development. Clearly the obstacles increase the greater the separation between the parents, not only in physical terms but also in terms of emotional distance between them. Taking into account that the best interests of the child should guide both parents' exercise of their responsibility, however, efforts should be made to ensure the greatest possible involvement by both parents in creating the enabling conditions.

2.6   'Others responsible for the child'

66. Many children do not have their own parents as caregivers. In the ideal family environment, intimate care can be taken almost for granted, but when it is absent there is need for special attention. When the strict requirements set out for adoption in Article 21 of the CRC have been followed, it may be assumed that the adopting parents recognize and implement the same responsibilities as the natural parents. With regard to foster parents, however, the situation may be less satisfactory, and vigilance is required. There is a great variation in local customs in the transfer of custody or guardianship of children. It is sometimes quite informal when relatives take over the care of children when their natural parents die, a phenomenon which has increased steeply in parts of Africa and elsewhere due to the

HIV/AIDS epidemic. Foster parents may themselves have limited ability and financial capacity to give proper care to the orphaned children. These are often neglected or outright exploited; some end up as prostitutes or street children.

67. State attention to the treatment of these children is therefore essential. Institutions may be required for orphaned or abandoned children, but it is broadly recognized that institutions housing many children are problematic in that it is difficult to ensure adequate care for each child. Foster placement, preferably with relatives of the deceased or disappeared parents, is generally to be preferred even if there are also considerable risks there involved. In the view of the CRC Committee, '[r]esearch suggests that low quality institutional care is unlikely to promote healthy physical and psychological development and can have serious negative consequences for long-term social adjustment, especially for children under three but also for children under five years old. To the extent that alternative care is required, early placement in family-based or family-like care is more likely to produce positive outcomes for young children. States Parties are encouraged to invest in and support forms of alternative care that can ensure security, continuity of care and affection, and the opportunity for young children to form long-term attachments based on mutual trust and respect; for example through fostering, adoption and support for members of extended families'.[44]

2.7   Social Trends and the Role of the Family

68. In the examination above on parental responsibility for the child's standard of living, there has been an underlying assumption about the ideal-type family, where parents and children live together in a stable relationship. Reality is much more complex. The roles of the family are changing in different parts of the world, though the changes do not necessarily go in the same directions. There are many positive developments, such as the outlawing of child marriages and an increase in knowledge of reproductive rights and attendant factors such as access to contraceptives. There are also more negative trends, including in many urbanized societies a strong increase in divorce and separation of the parents, very often with negative consequences for the child.

---

[44] CRC Committee, *General Comment No. 7, o.c.* (note 10), para. 31(c).

69. In some parts of the world, the spread of HIV/AIDS severely undermines or destroys conditions for family life because of the illness and death of one or more parents. Lack of local employment opportunities can also have a negative impact on the conditions of development for young children, for example, when one or both parents are forced to work far away from their families and their communities.

70. Parental ability to ensure adequate conditions for their child will therefore depend extensively on the overall level and nature of the development of the society concerned. Great variations exist between predominantly agricultural versus industrial or post-industrial societies. Even within the same State, a distinction must be drawn between the different cultural groups, including the distinction between the individualistic, market-oriented 'modern' society and the indigenous peoples within the same State which may have maintained cultural and societal traditions quite different from that of the majority society.

During periods of rapid social change, traditional practices may no longer be viable or relevant to present parental circumstances and lifestyles, but without sufficient time having elapsed for new practices to be assimilated, and for new parental competencies to be understood and valued.

3. Article 27(3): The Duty of the State to Assist

71. Article 27(3) reads: 'States Parties, in accordance with national conditions and within their means, shall take appropriate measures to assist parents and others responsible for the child to implement this right and shall in case of need provide material assistance and support programmes, particularly with regard to nutrition, clothing and housing'.

3.1 On Assistance to Parents versus Protection of the Child

72. While the parents and others responsible for the child have the primary responsibility for the implementation of the right of the child to an adequate standard of living, the State is under Article 27(3) required to assist them in doing so.

73. Before examining the nature of the assistance that should be provided, it may be useful to remember that States are also required to protect the child. Article 3(2) of the CRC requires States to ensure the child such protection

and care as is necessary for his or her well-being, taking into account the rights and duties of his or her parents, legal guardians, or other individuals legally responsible for him or her, and, to this end, States shall take all appropriate legislative and administrative measures. While protection of the child in many situations can be best promoted through assistance to parents, in some circumstances the child may have to be protected even against its own parents or other guardian. According to Article 19(1) of the CRC, States Parties shall take measures to protect the child from 'all forms of physical or mental violence, injury or abuse, neglect or negligent treatment, maltreatment or exploitation, including sexual abuse, *while in the care of parent(s), legal guardian(s) or any other person who has the care of the child.*'

74. In some cases there may be a difficult choice to be made whether to assist the parent(s) or guardian(s) to improve their implementation of the rights of the child, or to take measures for the protection of the child against the will of the parents. In the most serious cases, the protection of the child might ultimately consist in separating the child from its parent or guardian. The CRC Committee has warned against taking such a measure unless strictly justified in the best interest of the child. Protection of the child should not lead to the separation of the child from the parents, unless it is clearly in the child's interest to do so (Article 9 of the CRC).

The Committee has warned that young children are especially vulnerable to adverse consequences of separations because they are physically dependent on parents/primary caregivers, as well as emotionally attached to them. They are also least able to comprehend the circumstances of any separation. A separation might also lead to a placement of the child in institutions with low quality care.[45]

75. Where possible, the protection of the child should be combined with assistance and support for the parents. Article 19(2) provides that measures for the protection of the child 'should, as appropriate, include effective procedures for the establishment of social programmes to provide necessary support for the child and for those who have the care of the child' as well as for other forms of prevention and action. Measures adopted under Article 27(3) should create conditions that facilitate parents' efforts to secure the necessary conditions for the child. The measures should be constructive and sufficient to make it possible for the primary caregiver to implement

---

[45] CRC Committee, *General Comment No. 7, o.c.* (note 10), para. 15.

the child's right to an adequate standard of living, but the measures should not be too interventionist and thereby undermining the primary responsibility of the parents.

3.2   Requiring Indicators of Vulnerable Groups of Children

76. In its Guidelines for State Periodic Reporting, the CRC Committee requests States Parties to provide information on measures adopted to recognize and ensure the right of every child to a standard of living adequate for the child's physical, mental, spiritual, moral and social development. To be appropriate, the choice of measures requires solid knowledge of the situation facing different sets of children and their parents or other guardians. The CRC Committee therefore requests States Parties to provide information about the relevant indicators used to assess such as adequate standard of living, and its incidence among the child population, including by gender, age, region, rural/urban area, social and ethnic origin, and family situation.[46]

The Committee has recommended to States Parties to develop a comprehensive national strategy or national plan of action for children, and to give particular attention to identifying and giving priority to marginalized and disadvantaged groups.[47]

3.3   Poverty as an Overarching Problem

77. The CRC Committee has noted with concern that even the most basic standard of living is not assured for millions of young children, despite widespread recognition of the adverse consequences of deprivation:[48] 'Growing up in relative poverty undermines children's well-being, social inclusion and self-esteem and reduces opportunities for learning and development. Growing up in conditions of absolute poverty has even more serious consequences, threatening children's survival and their health, as well as undermining the basic quality of life. States parties are urged to implement systematic strategies to reduce poverty in early childhood as well as combat its negative effects on children's well-being. All possible means should be employed, including "material assistance and support programmes" for children and families (art. 27.3), in order to assure to young children a basic

---

[46] CRC Committee, *General Guidelines regarding the form and the contents of the periodic reports* (UN Doc. CRC/C/58, 1996) (hereinafter: CRC Committee, *Guidelines on State Periodic Reporting*), para. 103.

[47] CRC Committee, *General Comment No. 5, o.c.* (note 9), paras. 30 and 31.

[48] CRC Committee, *General Comment No. 7, o.c.* (note 10), para. 26.

standard of living consistent with rights. Implementing children's right to benefit from social security, including social insurance, is an important element of any strategy (art. 26).'[49]

In its concluding observations regarding some of the least-developed countries, the CRC Committee raises also the question of widespread corruption with its negative impact on the level of resources available for the implementation of the Convention. One such case is Togo. The Committee there also expressed its concern at the sharp decrease in public expenditure on education and health and at the lack of funds available for children living below the poverty line and for those in need of alternative care. The Committee therefore recommended that Togo should prioritize budgetary allocations to ensure implementation of the economic, social, cultural and other rights of children and to establish an integrated poverty reduction programme.[50]

But the problems may exist also in otherwise wealthy countries where inadequate attention is given to the need to assist poor families to ensure a standard of living adequate for the development of the child. One such example is the United Kingdom. In its Concluding Observations regarding the second report of that country, the Committee stated that it was 'extremely concerned at the high proportion of children living in poverty in the State party, which limits their enjoyment of many rights under the Convention and leads to a higher incidence among those children of death, accidents, pregnancy, poor housing and homelessness, malnutrition, educational failure and suicide.' The Committee urged the United Kingdom to take all necessary measures to the maximum of its available resources to accelerate the elimination of child poverty.[51]

In the so-called 'countries in transition', the former Socialist countries of Eastern Europe, there has been a marked trend to decrease the support for parents with children. The CRC Committee has expressed concern that the poor living conditions seriously limited the children's enjoyment of their rights in the family. The Committee has therefore recommended that these States take all necessary measures to provide support and material assistance to economically disadvantaged families, including targeted programmes

---

[49] Ibid.
[50] CRC Committee, *Concluding Observations: Togo* (CRC/C/15/Add.255, 2005), paras. 17 and 18.
[51] CRC Committee, *Concluding Observations: United Kingdom* (CRC/C/15/Add.188, 2002), paras. 45 and 46.

with regard to the most vulnerable groups of families, in order to guarantee the right of all children to an adequate standard of living.[52]

3.4 '[I]n case of need provide material assistance and support programmes, particularly with regard to nutrition, clothing and housing'

78. The CESCR Committee has adopted general comments on the obligations of States in regard to food and nutrition and to housing. In its General Comment 4 on the Right to Housing, adopted in 1991, the Committee has spelled out in some detail what is required to consider the housing 'adequate'[53] and has argued that a national housing strategy is required which defines the objectives for the development of shelter conditions, identifies the resources available to meet these goals and the most cost-effective way of using them and sets out the responsibilities and time-frame for the implementation of the necessary measures. Priority must be given to social groups living in unfavourable conditions.[54] It is not required that the housing deficit is met by the building of houses by the State. 'The promotion by States parties of "enabling strategies", combined with a full commitment to obligations under the right to adequate housing, should thus be encouraged. In essence, the obligation is to demonstrate that, in aggregate, the measures being taken are sufficient to realize the right for every individual in the shortest possible time in accordance with the maximum of available resources'.[55]

In its General Comment on the Right to Adequate Food and Nutrition,[56] the CESCR Committee has observed that, despite the fact that the international community has frequently reaffirmed the importance of full respect for the right to adequate food, a disturbing gap still exists in many parts of the world. 'More than 840 million people throughout the world, most of them in developing countries, are chronically hungry; millions of people are suffering from famine as the result of natural disasters, the increasing incidence of civil strife and wars in some regions and the use of food as a political weapon'. The Committee also observed that while the problems of hunger and malnutrition are often particularly acute in developing countries,

---

[52] See, *e.g.*: CRC Committee, *Concluding Observations: Russian Federation* (CRC/C/15/Add.274, 2005), paras. 62 and 63.
[53] CESCR Committee, *General Comment No. 4, o.c.* (note 14), para. 8.
[54] *Ibid.*, paras. 9–13.
[55] *Ibid.*, para. 14.
[56] CESCR Committee, *General Comment No. 12, o.c.* (note 16).

malnutrition, under-nutrition and other problems which relate to the right
to adequate food and the right to freedom from hunger, also exist in some
of the most economically developed countries. Fundamentally, the roots
of the problem of hunger and malnutrition are not lack of food but lack of
access to available food, *inter alia* because of poverty, by large segments of
the world's population.

The Committee called on States to adopt a national strategy to ensure the
enjoyment for all of the right to food, and pointed out that the it would be
a violation of the CESCR when a State failed to ensure the satisfaction of,
at the very least, the minimum essential level required to be free from
hunger: 'Should a State party argue that resource constraints make it impos-
sible to provide access to food for those who are unable by themselves to
secure such access, the State has to demonstrate that every effort has been
made to use all the resources at its disposal in an effort to satisfy, as a matter of priority, those minimum obligations. This follows from Article 2.1
of the Covenant, which obliges a State party to take the necessary steps to
the maximum of its available resources, as previously pointed out by the
Committee in its General Comment No. 3, paragraph 10. A State claiming
that it is unable to carry out its obligation for reasons beyond its control
therefore has the burden of proving that this is the case and that it has
unsuccessfully sought to obtain international support to ensure the availability and accessibility of the necessary food.'[57]

3.5 *Assisting Parents and Others to Increase their Ability to Implement the Child's Right to a Standard Adequate for its Development*

79. The CRC Committee has recommended that assistance to parents should
include education and counselling of parents and supportive services for
mothers, fathers, siblings, grandparents and others who from time to time
may be responsible for promoting the child's best interests. Assistance should
also include offering support to parents and other family members in ways
that encourage positive and sensitive relationships with young children and
enhance understanding of children's rights and best interests.[58]

A significant assistance to parents consists in healthcare services and the
availability of educational institutions for the child. The CRC Committee has

---

[57] *Ibid.*, para. 17.
[58] CRC Committee, *General Comment No. 7* para. 20 (c).

called on State Parties to ensure that parents are given appropriate support to enable them to involve young children fully in such programmes, especially the most disadvantaged and vulnerable groups.[59]

Many parents have fulltime jobs on which their economy and the livelihood of the child depend. They are faced with difficulties in combining this with their parental responsibilities. Article 18(3) of the CRC requires States Parties to take all appropriate measures to ensure that children of working parents have the right to benefit from childcare services and other facilities. Wherever possible, affordable, appropriate and reliable kindergartens should be available to assist the parents to reconcile their responsibility for their child with the livelihood of the family as a whole. In this connection, the CRC Committee recommends that States Parties ratify the Maternity Protection Convention, 2000 (No. 183) of the International Labour Organization.[60]

3.6   *Parents and Guardians in Particularly Vulnerable Situations*

80. Difficult problems arise when the *parents*, or one of them (particularly the mother) are themselves children *below eighteen*. Both the CEDAW Committee and the CRC Committee have strongly recommended States that have not already done so to increase the minimum age for marriage to eighteen, and to develop and implement programmes that provide access to sexual and reproductive health services, including family planning and contraception, to avoid pregnancy for girls below that age. Taking into account, however, that child marriages are still widespread particularly in rural areas in many developing countries, and that adolescent mothers may be prone to depression and anxiety compromising their ability to care for the child, the CRC Committee has recommended States to foster positive and supportive attitudes towards the adolescent parents, in order for them to care for their children.

81. States should give particular attention to the situation of *children affected and orphaned by HIV/AIDS.* The CRC Committee has pointed out that consistent with their obligations under Article 27 of the Convention, States Parties must support and strengthen the capacity of families and communities of children orphaned by AIDS to provide them with a standard of living

---

[59] CRC Committee, *General Comment No. 7, o.c.* (note 10), paras. 20 and 21.
[60] *Ibid.*, para. 21.

adequate for their physical, mental, spiritual, moral, economic and social development, including access to psychosocial care, as needed.[61]

82. Parents having responsibility for *disabled children* should be given particular support to facilitate their efforts to ensure to the child equal opportunities for an adequate standard of living.[62] Support services, including assistive devices should therefore be made available for persons with disabilities.[63]

Migrant workers are often having greater difficulty in finding work and an acceptable standard of living. It is therefore particularly important to support them in their effort to ensure that the children do not suffer. One such case is that of Norway, which generally has a high standard of living for the general population. The CRC Committee noted with concern the high proportion of immigrant children living in households with a persistently low income and recommended that Norway should ensure that the needs of all children are met and to take all necessary measures to ensure that no group of children live under the poverty line.[64]

83. In many parts of Europe but particularly in Central and Eastern Europe, the *Roma* face particular difficulties and are rarely integrated in a satisfactory way in the economic life of the country. The CRC Committee has noted that many Roma children end up as street children. Many of them do not attend schools and a high percentage among them are ill. In the case of Bosnia-Herzegovina, the Committee therefore recommended that street children should be provided with adequate nutrition, clothing, housing, health-care and educational opportunities, including vocational and life-skills training, in order to support their full development.[65]

84. In some Asian countries, in particular India, severe poverty and social inequalities are caused by *'untouchability'* and caste- and tribe-motivated abuse. This causes persistent and significant social discrimination of children belonging to Scheduled Castes and Tribes and other tribal groups. The

---

[61] CRC Committee, *General Comment No. 3*, *o.c.* (note 12), para. 33.
[62] CRC Committee, *General Comment No. 4*, *o.c.* (note 28), para. 36(d).
[63] CESCR Committee, *General Comment No. 5*, *o.c.* (note 17), para. 30.
[64] CRC Committee, *Concluding Observations: Norway* (UN Doc. CRC/C/15/Add.263, 2005), paras. 37 and 38.
[65] CRC Committee, *Concluding Observations: Bosnia and Herzegovina* (UN Doc. CRC/C/15/Add.260, 2005), para. 66.

CRC Committee has therefore urged the State Party to advance and protect these groups.[66]

3.7   Responsibilities for Separated and Unaccompanied Children outside their Country

85. In September 2005, the CRC Committee issued its General Comment 6 to draw attention to the particularly vulnerable situation of unaccompanied and separated children and to provide guidance on the protection, care and proper treatment of such children. The Committee has observed that an increasing number of children have come into such situations, due to persecution of the child or the parents; international conflict and civil war; trafficking in various contexts and forms, including sale by parents; the search for better economic opportunities, and other factors. Such children face greater risks of, *inter alia*, sexual exploitation and abuse, military recruitment, child labour (including for their foster families) and detention, and are often discriminated against and denied access to food, shelter, housing, health services and education.

State obligations under the CRC apply to each child within the State's territory and to all children subject to its jurisdiction (Article 2), and cannot be arbitrarily and unilaterally curtailed either by excluding zones or areas from a State's territory or by defining particular zones or areas as not, or only partly, under the jurisdiction of the State. The enjoyment of rights stipulated in the Convention is not limited to children who are citizens of a State Party and must therefore, if not explicitly stated otherwise in the Convention, also be available to all children – including asylum-seeking, refugee and migrant children – irrespective of their nationality, immigration status or statelessness.[67]

The Committee recommends that States appoint a guardian as soon as the unaccompanied or separated child is identified. Guardianship should regularly be assigned to the accompanying adult family member or non-primary family caretaker unless there is an indication that it would not be in the best interests of the child to do so, for example, where the accompanying adult has abused the child. In cases where a child is accompanied by a non-family adult or caretaker, suitability for guardianship must be scrutinized

---

[66] CRC Committee, *Concluding Observations: India* (UN Doc. CRC/C/15/Add. 228, 2004), para. 28.
[67] CRC Committee, *General Comment No. 6, o.c.* (note 11), para. 12.

more closely. If such a guardian is able and willing to provide day-to-day care, but unable to adequately represent the child's best interests in all spheres and at all levels of the child's life, supplementary measures (such as the appointment of an adviser or legal representative) must be secured.

86. In fulfilment of their obligations under Article 27(3) to ensure that separated and unaccompanied children have a standard of living adequate for their physical, mental, spiritual and moral development, States shall provide material assistance and support programmes, particularly with regard to nutrition, clothing and housing. Where their capacity to do so is limited, they should accept and facilitate the assistance offered by UNICEF, UNESCO, UNHCR and other UN agencies and where appropriate, other competent intergovernmental organizations or non-governmental organisations to secure an adequate standard of living for unaccompanied and separated children.[68]

4. Article 27(4): recovery of Maintenance for the Child

87. Under Article 27(4), States Parties are requested to take all appropriate measures to secure the recovery of maintenance for the child from the parents or other persons having financial responsibility for the child, both within the State Party and from abroad. In particular, where the person having financial responsibility for the child lives in a State different from that of the child, States Parties shall promote the accession to international agreements or the conclusion of such agreements, as well as the making of other appropriate arrangements.

4.1   Travaux préparatoires and Information Requested by the CRC Committee

88. During the drafting of Article 27 of the CRC, Australia referred to and supported an NGO proposal to the effect that the responsibilities of parents or guardians, including that of providing appropriate support for the child, continued even when the child lives apart from them. This was opposed on the ground that it was already covered by Article 27(2) and (3). Australia then suggested the addition to 27(2) that the responsibility continued even when parents are living apart from the child. This was considered unnecessary as being implicit in the exiting text of Article 27(2). The observer from

---

[68] *Ibid.*, paras. 43 and 44.

Finland argued that the main problem to be addressed was the situation where one or both parents lived in countries different from where the child lived, and that measures should be adopted to ensure the effective recovery of maintenance from abroad.

In the following discussion it was suggested that the principle of recovery should be a general one, involving not only parents or other persons having financial responsibility who lived abroad, but also persons who lived within the territory but avoided maintenance of the child. The final text quoted above therefore covers both situations.[69]

89. In its Guidelines for State Periodic Reporting regarding recovery of maintenance for the child, the CRC Committee calls on the States Parties to indicate the measures adopted (including legislative, administrative and judicial measures) and mechanisms or programmes developed to secure the recovery of maintenance for the child from the parents or other persons having financial responsibility for the child, both within the State and from abroad, including in cases of the separation or divorce of the parents.[70]

Information should also be provided on measures taken to ensure the maintenance of the child in cases where parents or other persons having financial responsibility for the child evade the payment of such maintenance. Information is also requested on measures to ensure respect for the general principles of the Convention, namely non-discrimination, the best interests of the child, respect for the views of the child and the right to life, survival and development to the maximum extent, and on factors and difficulties which may have affected the recovery of maintenance for the child (for example, lack of birth registration) or the enforcement of decisions concerning maintenance obligations. The Committee requests relevant disaggregated data in this area, including by gender, age, national origin and place of residence of the child and his or her parents, or of the persons financially responsible for him or her.[71]

The Committee also calls for information on relevant international agreements the State has concluded or to which it has acceded, as well as any other appropriate arrangement it has made.[72]

---

[69] S. Detrick, *o.c.* (note 1), pp. 464–465.
[70] CRC Committee, *Guidelines on State Periodic Reporting*, para. 79.
[71] *Ibid.*
[72] *Ibid.*; *cf. infra* No. 98.

4.2   *Shared Responsibility and the Context Where this Gives Rise to Problems*

90. As stated above, the primary responsibility of the parents implies that they do have a responsibility and that it can and must be enforced.[73] As provided for in Article 18 of the CRC, it is a shared responsibility to which both parents must contribute. Both parents shall bear the expenses for the upbringing, support and education of the child, according to the child's ability and aptitude and the financial circumstances of the parents. If persons other than the parents have been assigned parental responsibility, then these persons have the same obligations to support the child. Support primarily encompasses expenses for food, clothing and housing, child care and leisure activities. The level of support must be adjusted to the parents' finances. It is, however, necessary that certain minimum support requirements be fulfilled.

91. The responsibility to maintain the child is a right of the child. No one can renounce that right. In practice, problems arise which Article 27 is intended to cover. It may arise even if the parents are married and live together, if one of the parents refuses to contribute to the maintenance of the child. The probability of such refusal increases if the parents divorce or otherwise split apart, and it becomes particularly difficult to handle if the parent who evades payment lives in a country different from that of the child. In some cases, the problem is not necessarily a total refusal to contribute but a much lower contribution than what is reasonable in light of the needs of the child and the parent's financial capability.

4.3   *Precondition: Ensuring that Parenthood is Recognized and that both Parents are Held Responsible*

92. The question of maintenance contribution on the basis of parenthood requires that the parenthood is recognized. If the child is born to a married couple living together this does not normally raise problems, provided the child is registered at birth. Under Article 7 of the CRC, every child shall be registered immediately after birth and shall have the right to know and be cared for by his or her parents. This right is extensively violated. In large parts of the developing world, many children are not registered. In rural areas of many African and Asian countries less than half of the children are registered at birth. When a married parent subsequently leaves the family,

---

[73] *Cf. supra* No. 46–49.

the problem of identifying responsibility for maintenance is sometimes insurmountable.

As one example: in the case of India, the CRC Committee expressed its deep concern that as much as 46 percent of children were not registered at birth. Similar concerns have been expressed in regard to many countries in Africa and Asia.[74]

The lack of registration is particularly extensive within marginalised groups, such as indigenous peoples and various kinds of vulnerable minorities. In several European countries it affects in particular the Roma populations. It is aggravated by the fact that primary health care, including mother and child health care centres, is often not accessible by the women in marginalized groups, due to inability to pay the fee or for other reasons. Registration is otherwise often linked with the care provided at such centres.

93. In all parts of the world, the situation is even more difficult regarding non-marital children.[75] When the child is born to an unmarried mother, the determination of the parenthood of the father has traditionally been difficult. In our time it is technically easier due to the use of DNA identification, but its application can still give rise to practical difficulties. It should at all times be kept in mind, however, that the right to maintenance from both parents is a right of the child and it should be enforced without any discrimination between marital and non-marital children. The mother cannot renounce the right on behalf of the child. The fact that the father does not live with and has never lived with the mother is no justification for evasion of maintenance. Non-discrimination requires equalisation of maintenance between marital and non-marital children. Article 27(2) combined with Article 18(1) must be understood to oblige States to ensure the recognition and identification of parenthood. They impose an obligation

---

[74] CRC Committee, *Concluding Observations: India* (UN Doc. CRC/C/15/Add.288, 2004), para. 38.
[75] In MARCKX v. BELGIUM, (Application number 00006833/74, 1979) the ECtHR confirmed, on the basis of ECHR Article 8 in combination with Article 14, the right of the child of an unmarried mother to recognition of its maternal affiliation from the moment of birth and without further formalities, with the legal consequences flowing from such affiliation including inheritance rights. It referred to the principle that "mater semper certa est" (there can be no doubt regarding who is the mother). The question of paternal affiliation for children of unmarried parents was not an issue in the case, but legislation was at that time already adopted or in preparation in many European countries, including Belgium, to reform of the provisions on the establishment of paternity to ensure equal responsibility for both parents.

on natural fathers to provide maintenance, also when they do not live together. The right set out in Article 7 of the CRC of the child to know the parents is also a right to know who the father is even if the child is born outside wedlock.

The CRC Committee has faced this problem in regard to a number of countries. In regard to Algeria, *e.g.*, the Committee has in its Concluding Observations expressed its concern that children born out of wedlock are not entitled to equal rights, such as to be recognized as a 'legitimate' child of the father. The Committee has therefore recommended that States revise relevant national family law to ensure that men and women have equal parental responsibilities, regardless of their marital status, and to abolish the discriminatory classification of children as 'illegitimate'.[76]

94. It is a matter of considerable concern that men having intercourse with women from marginalized or discriminated groups evade payment of maintenance for children that might result from such relations, and that governments do not effectively ensure that parenthood is identified and recognized and that payment is enforced.

4.4   Ensuring Maintenance and Determining the Scope and Amount

95. Assuming that the responsible parent or other person responsible for the child has been identified, the next task is to ensure that maintenance is paid for the child and that the amount is determined. In the case of divorce, this is often a part of divorce proceedings. In cases of contested fatherhood it is part of the process determining who is the father and therefore responsible.

Where the fatherhood is not in dispute, it is desirable that the process of determining the duty to pay maintenance and the size of the payment is made simple so that it does not by itself require inordinately long and costly procedures. In some countries the social security offices act in the capacity of maintenance enforcement officer. The maintenance enforcement officer shall ensure recovery when requested by the person entitled to the payments.

---

[76] CRC Committee, *Concluding observations: Algeria* (UN Doc. CRC/C/15/Add.69, 2005), paras. 43 and 44.

The costs of recovery which are not covered by the person who makes the maintenance payments can then be covered by the public authorities.

96. The scope of maintenance should be determined by dividing the cost of maintaining the child proportionately between the parents according to their income. The amount of maintenance would then be tested against the ability to pay of the person required to pay maintenance. The maintenance regulations should ensure equality between parents and encourage both parents to care for their children.

97. In order to find the person who is responsible it may be necessary to release information about the whereabouts of debtors to ensure they pay, and to have available sanctions against recalcitrant debtors who refuse to pay. This can include deduction of maintenance contribution from the salary of employed persons.

4.5   When the Reluctant Parent Lives Abroad

98. When the parents live in different countries, or the children live in a country different than that of one (or both) of the parents or others responsible for the child, particular difficulties arise. These are in part of a practical nature and in part legal. There may be differences in the law between the countries regarding payment of maintenance. Article 27(4) of the CRC therefore requires States Parties to promote the accession to international agreements or the conclusion of such agreements, as well as the making of other appropriate arrangements. There is not yet in existence any such agreements with a global reach, but numerous arrangements have been made by some countries, both bilaterally, regionally and wider.

Among the regional arrangements are the 1988 Lugano Convention on Judicial Competence and on the Enforcement of Judicial Decisions in Private Law, primarily open to the member countries of the European Community (EC) and the European Free Trade Area (EFTA), containing provisions for the enforcements of judgements referring, among other things, to maintenance allowances. The Council of Europe has also adopted a Regulation on jurisdiction and the enforcement of judgements in civil law, adopted in 2000 and entered into force on 1 March 2002. A wider reach is foreseen in the UN Convention of 20 June 1956 on the Recovery Abroad of Maintenance and the Hague Conventions of 15 April 1958 and 2 October 1973 on the Recognition and Enforcement of Decisions Concerning Maintenance Obligations.

The main points in such arrangements is that a decision rendered in one contracting State shall be recognised or enforced in another contracting State if rendered by an authority considered to have jurisdiction in accordance to that agreement. The authority of the State addressed shall be bound by the findings of fact on which the authority of the State of origin based its jurisdiction.

CHAPTER FOUR

SHARED INTERNATIONAL RESPONSIBILITY?

99. The CRC is primarily addressed to States, who by becoming parties under-take obligations to respect, protect and fulfil the rights to all children living within their territory. See Article 2(1) of the CRC: '*States Parties* shall respect and ensure the rights set forth in the present Convention to each child within their jurisdiction . . .' and the first sentence of Article 4: '*States Parties shall undertake* all appropriate legislative, administrative, and other measures for the implementation of the rights recognized in the present Convention'.[77]

100. Article 4 adds, however, the following in its second sentence: 'With regard to economic, social and cultural rights, States Parties shall under-take such measures to the maximum extent of their available resources and, where needed, *within the framework of international co-operation*'.[78]

101. In light of the current situation of children world wide, the task would be overwhelming if it was to be achieved solely on the efforts by the devel-oping countries themselves. The least developed countries in particular would have no hope within the near future to meet the obligations envis-aged for them under Article 27(3) to assist the parents in ensuring an ade-quate standard for the development of all children within their jurisdiction.

The total number of children (persons below 18) in the world are a little over 2.2 billion. The overwhelming majority of them (1.93 billion or 88 per cent) live in the developing countries.[79] Poverty and insecurity affect hun-dreds of millions of children whose conditions are far below the standards adequate for their development. The causes are multiple: diseases such as malaria and HIV/AIDS, internal conflicts, legacies of past colonialism and racial discrimination. Bad governance and corruption is one factor, private

---

[77] Emphasis added by the author.
[78] Emphasis added by the author.
[79] UNICEF gives in its *State of the World 2005* (note 3) the numbers of children (persons under 18) in 2003 to 1,924,210,000 in the developing countries out of a world total of children set at 2,183,635,000.

greed and corporate accumulation of wealth is another. Even well intentioned development projects, while improving the lot for some part of the population, can lead to further impoverishment of others parts of society.

Much of the blame can be placed at the State in which the child lives, and on cultural traditions and institutions within their own society which are barriers to the full development of all children. Traditions of caste and racial or ethnic discrimination block millions of children from reaching an adequate standard of life. Discrimination of women remains widespread. Child marriages and early pregnancies cause many parents to be unable to ensure an adequate standard. Denial of reproductive rights for women, including barriers to access or use of contraception, prevent them from ensuring sufficient spacing of their children, and cause them to be unable to provide the necessary care and support for the many children they bear. Evasion by one of the parents of the duty to contribute to the maintenance of the child is one of the causes at the personal level.

If all States fully implemented the CEDAW, including their duty to modify cultural practices based on notions of inferiority or superiority between women and men (Article 5 of the CEDAW) and their duty to ensure that women could enjoy their right to decide freely and responsibly on the number and spacing of their children and to have access to the information, education and means to enable them to exercise these rights (Article 16(e) of the CEDAW); if all States also fully implemented the Convention on the Elimination of Racial Discrimination, including the effective elimination of discrimination on the grounds of caste; if the exercise of government was carried out in a transparent and accountable way, and States fulfilled their duty to realize the economic, social and cultural rights to the maximum of their available resources (Article 2 of the CESCR) we would come a long way towards conditions for ensuring to every child an adequate standard of living.

102. When all this is said, however, it is also clear that many developing countries do not have the resources and capacity on their own to secure for all children within their territory an adequate standard of living. Whatever the reasons for this shortcoming, international cooperation and assistance to ensure the rights in a meaningful way is necessary and will have to remain so for a considerable period of time.

Referring to Article 4 of the CRC, the CRC Committee has pointed out that '[...] implementation of the Convention is a cooperative exercise for the

States of the world'. This article and others in the CRC highlight the need for international cooperation. The UN Charter (Articles 55 and 56) identifies the overall purposes of international economic and social cooperation, and members pledge themselves under the Charter "to take joint and separate action in cooperation with the Organization' to achieve these purposes".[80]

103. Through multilateral agencies and funds, States do to some extent meet their international responsibility in this field. The CRC Committee has called on all UN and UN-related agencies in their promotion of international cooperation and technical assistance to be guided by the Convention and to mainstream children's rights throughout their activities. The agencies should also seek to ensure within their influence that international cooperation is targeted at supporting States to fulfil their obligations under the Convention.[81]

Effective international cooperation can also strengthen capacity-building for early childhood, in terms of policy development, programme development, research, and professional training. Through these efforts, State priorities may be improved in favour of the child, and the administrative capacity and skill to address these tasks can be improved.

Among the agencies most directly involved is the United Nations International Children's Emergency Fund, UNICEF. It was established on 11 December 1946 by the UN to meet the emergency needs of children in post-war Europe and China. In 1950, its mandate was broadened to address the long-term needs of children and women in developing countries everywhere. UNICEF became a permanent part of the UN system in 1953, when its name was shortened to the United Nations Children's Fund, but UNICEF retained its original acronym. It has made the CRC the point of reference for its work.

The CRC Committee has endorsed the aims of the 20/20 initiative, to achieve universal access to basic social services of good quality on a sustainable basis, as a shared responsibility of developing and donor States.[82]

104. The least developed countries and several other developing countries are unable to provide sufficient assistance to parents or others responsible for the child to ensure an adequate standard of living for every child within

---

[80] CRC Committee, *General Comment No. 5, o.c.* (note 9), para. 60.
[81] *Ibid.*, para. 64.
[82] *Ibid.*, para. 62.

their jurisdiction. The CRC Committee has therefore encouraged the efforts being made to reduce poverty in the most heavily indebted countries through the Poverty Reduction Strategy Papers (PRSP) and has pointed out that as the central, country-led strategy for achieving the millennium development goals, PRSPs must include a strong focus on children's rights. The Committee urges Governments, donors and civil society to ensure that children are a prominent priority in the development of PRSPs and sectorwide approaches to development (SWAps). Both PRSPs and SWAps should reflect children's rights principles, with a holistic, child-centred approach recognizing children as holders of rights and the incorporation of development goals and objectives which are relevant to children.[83]

105. The limited financial and other material resources require more than technical assistance, however. The CRC Committee has noted that international meetings held to review progress have concluded that many States are going to have difficulty meeting fundamental economic and social rights unless additional resources are allocated and efficiency in resource allocation is increased. Through the commitments made in the UN Millennium Declaration and at other global meetings, including the UN General Assembly Special Session on Children,[84] States have pledged themselves, in particular, to international cooperation to eliminate poverty.

The improvement of conditions for an adequate standard of living depends heavily on the willingness of developed countries and their financial institutions to ensure that conditions are created by which the developing countries can build up their resources to meet these tasks, be it by transfer of resources or other measures which improve the resource position of developing countries in the global economy. The CRC Committee has called on the World Bank Group, the International Monetary Fund and World Trade Organisation to ensure that their activities related to international cooperation and economic development give primary consideration to the best interests of children and promote full implementation of the Convention.[85]

More specifically the CRC Committee called on donor institutions, including the World Bank, other UN institutions and bilateral donors to support

---

[83] CRC Committee, *General Comment No. 5, o.c.* (note 9), para. 62.
[84] See http://www.unicef.org/specialsession.
[85] CRC Committee, *General Comment No. 5, o.c.* (note 9), para. 64.

early childhood development programmes financially and technically, as one of their main targets to assist sustainable development in countries benefiting from international assistance.[86] It has advised States Parties that the Convention should form the framework for international development assistance related directly or indirectly to children and that programmes of donor States should be rights-based, and it urges States to meet internationally agreed targets, including the UN target for international development assistance of 0.7 per cent of gross domestic product, and encourages States parties that receive international aid and assistance to allocate a substantive part of that aid specifically to children. The CRC Committee expects States parties to be able to identify on a yearly basis the amount and proportion of international support earmarked for the implementation of children's rights.[87]

---

[86] CRC Committee, *General Comment No. 7, o.c.* (note 10), para. 42.
[87] CRC Committee, *General Comment No. 5, o.c.* (note 9), para. 61.